DAD JOKES

Bad Jokes and Puns Inspired by Dads!

Jack Duncan

ISBN-10: 1539751848

ISBN-13: 978-1539751847

CONTENTS

INTRODUCTION

Everybody appreciates a good dad joke.

Dad jokes are friendly little jokes that the whole family can enjoy, often focusing on puns and wordplay.

Some people enjoy them because they find them to be genuinely funny, while others enjoy them because they can't believe just how awful they are!

Over the years, dad's have perfected the art of this inoffensive, positive style of joke as a way of entertaining both adults and kids alike.

This book honors this style of humor by offering some of the best dad jokes around, guaranteed to make everyone you know either laugh or roll their eyes!

JOKES

1

Why didn't the dad take his trash out for the waste collectors?

They'd already *bin and gone!*

2

Why did the banker-dad have to quit his job?

He *lost interest*!

3

Why did the dog refuse to go for walks in the forest?

He was scared of the tree's *bark!*

4

How did the Arabian dad make himself less visible in the desert?

Camel-flage!

5

Why don't dads ever starve in deserts?

They eat the *sand which is* there!

6

Why did the dad bank manager leave a root vegetable in the vault when he heard someone was plotting to rob his bank?

It was a *turnip for the crooks!*

7

Why did the dad use as little wood as possible when building an extension on his house?

He wanted to *conserve-a-tree*!

8

What did the dad bartender say when a customer asked for a refund on his beer?

This is the *pint of no return!*

9

What is a dad's favorite breakfast in bed?

Two *rolls* and a *turnover!*

10

What do you call an old snowman?

Water!

11

Why did the bored dad decide to make some spaghetti?

He wanted to *pasta* time away!

12

Which hand is it better to write with?

Neither, it's best to write with a pen!

13

What's purple and 5000 miles long?

The *Grape* Wall of China!

14

How did the stupid dad get time off of work?

He applied for *thick leave!*

15

What did the dad bailiff who moonlighted as a bartender serve?

Subpoena coladas!

16

What did they name the film about a dad who had amazing revelations while eating his cereal?

Breakfast *Epiphanies!*

17

Why did the dad sit on his watch?

He wanted to be *on time!*

18

What did the dad woodworkers do when they weren't happy with their union?

They former a *splinter* group!

19

What happened when 19 and 20 got into a fight?

21!

20

Why do you go to bed every night?

Because the bed won't come to you!

21

What's the worst thing about having a dad who is a nervous guitar player?

They're always *fretting* about something!

22

What do you call a rich elf?

Welfy!

23

Why did the robber take a bath before he stole from the bank?

He wanted to make a *clean get away!*

24

Why was the detective duck given an award?

Because he *quacked* the case!

25

What did the dad do when his daughter's doll
lost a leg?

Took it to the *plastic surgeon!*

26

Who are the target market of Elvis Presley-themed steakhouses?

People who love *meat tender!*

27

Why didn't the sun go to university?

Because it already had a *million degrees!*

28

I changed my iPod's name to Titanic..

It's currently *synching!*

29

What do bee-dads do in the winter?

Hivernate!

30

What streets do ghosts haunt?

Dead ends!

31

Why did the horse move stables?

He couldn't stand the *neigh*-bours!

32

What do you call a group of singing killer whales?

An *orca-stra!*

33

Why do dad swimming teams always win their races?

They're good at *pooling* their efforts!

34

What happened when the weatherman-dad broke both his arms and legs?

He had *four casts!*

35

Why did the dad buy a deck of cards when he started his new office job?

He was told he would need *four suits!*

36

I stayed up all night to see where the sun went..

Then it *dawned* on me!

37

What shape would you find at the bottom of the Bermuda Triangle?

A *wreck*-tangle!

38

Want to hear a pizza joke?

Nevermind, it's too *cheesy!*

39

Boss: You missed work yesterday, didn't you?

Dad: *Not really!*

40

Why are the police in a hurry to catch the dad who robbed people by threatening them with a lighted match?

They want to catch him before he *strikes again!*

41

What do you call a knight who is afraid to fight?

Sir Render!

42

What did the man who sent his girlfriend a
huge pile of snow ask her?

Did you get my *drift*?

43

How does a dad cut a wave in a half?

With a *sea saw!*

44

How did the police end up catching the dad who was on the run in the bathroom?

He stood on a set of scales and *gave himself a weigh!*

45

Who's in charge of the pencil case?

The *ruler!*

46

What happened to the missing carpenter-dad?

He *varnished* without a trace!

47

Why did the dad have to quit his job as a fisherman?

He was suffering from too much *pier pressure!*

48

What did the dad say when he was told he would have trouble growing bananas because of the climate?

"I want to grow it, not *climb it!*"

49

Why don't any Saudi Arabian's suffer with mental illness?

There are *nomad* people there!

50

Why was the dadfish unhappy with his son's report card?

Because all of his grades were *under C!*

51

If a crocodile makes shoes, what does a banana make?

Slippers!

52

What did the Buddhist dad say to the hot-dog seller?

Make me one with everything!

53

What did the dad farmer use to move his sleeping cattle?

A bulldozer!

54

What did the dad say when he was asked if all of his warm-weather clothes were comfortable?

Summer!

55

Where do books sleep?

Under their *covers!*

56

Doctors claim there are over six million
overweight people in the world..

These are, of course, only *round figures*!

57

What is a dad's favorite type of key?

Cookies!

58

What happened when the glassblower-dad accidentally inhaled?

He got a *pane* in the stomach!

59

What do you call an elephant in a phone booth?

Stuck!

60

How did the dad realize that the bucket was sick?

It became *a little pale!*

61

What does a nomadic tree do when it gets bored?

It packs its *trunk* and *leaves!*

62

Why do fish live in salt water?

Because pepper makes them sneeze!

63

What does a computer do at lunchtime?

Have a *byte!*

64

What do you call a well behaved pet snake
that works for the government?

A civil *serpent!*

65

What happened when the dad wasn't paying
attention during the turn of the millennium
celebrations?

It went in one era 'n out the other!

66

What do dad-birds give out on Halloween?

Tweets!

67

Why did people get bored of talking to the monorail enthusiast?

He had a *one-track mind!*

68

An archaeologist in Britain found an ancient door..

It had a *stone hinge* on it!

69

What did the dad-politician do when he was told he had to slash the budget?

He held a fund *razor!*

70

Do sticks float in the sea?

They *would!*

71

How do you keep a bull from charging?

Take away its credit card!

72

I did a theatrical performance about puns..

It was a *play on words*!

73

What's Irish and stays out all night?

Paddy O'Furniture!

74

How does a train eat?

Chew chew!

75

How can you tell when a Korean person is a vampire?

They don't have a *Seoul!*

76

What does a backwards poet write?

Inverse!

77

What do you do if you want to buy chess pieces?

Contact a *pawn broker!*

78

Why didn't the dad-rabbit trust the comb?

Because he heard it *teased hares!*

79

Why was the banker dad so devastated when he left the door unlocked and the bank got burgled?

It was all his *vault!*

80

What did the dad do when his kleptomania was acting up?

He *took something for it!*

81

What happened when the dad accidentally backed into a menorah on the first day of Hanukkah?

He *burned his end at both candles*!

82

What happened when the dad bicycle salesman broke his ankle?

He struggled to *peddle his wares!*

83

What did the dad-judge say when the skunk walked into the court room?

***Odor* in the court!**

84

Why are archaeologist-dads so angry?

They always have a *bone to pick!*

85

What did the archaeologist-dad say when he accidentally broke his friend's newly discovered artifact?

It looks like I owe you *anthrapology!*

86

How does a hunter-dad catch a train?

He follows its *tracks!*

87

What do you call a smart group of trees?

A *brainforest!*

88

I used to think I was indecisive..

..but now I'm not so sure!

89

Why did the cantaloupe jump into the river?

It wanted to be a *watermelon!*

90

What flower do you have on your face?

Two-lips!

91

What did the dad say when he saw a man and a woman wrapped in a barcode?

Are you two an *item*?

92

What does reading while sunbathing make you?

Well-*read!*

93

What do you call a pig with no friends?

A *boar!*

94

Why are pirates called pirates?

Cause they *arrrrr!*

95

What kind of aftershave does a dad genetic scientists wear?

Eau de *clone!*

96

What did the Englishman in court plead when he was charged with stealing ducks?

Not guilty, *Mallard!*

97

Why did the dad buy his wife a pack of playing cards for their anniversary?

She said she wanted something with a lot of *diamonds* in it!

98

Did you read the newspaper article about the raisin who cheated on his wife?

It was in the *current affairs* section!

99

Why did the dad attach two snakes to the front of his car?

He needed some window *vipers!*

100

Why didn't the kids want to go to the Coca-Cola factory?

Because of the *pop quiz*!

101

Why did the prospector-dad refuse to smoke dynamite?

He was afraid it would *blow his mind!*

102

What did the dad give the manager when he was served cold food at the Italian restaurant?

A *pizza* his mind!

103

Mom: I hope I didn't just see you eating my last slice of cake!

Dad: *I hope you didn't either!*

104

My friend Max hates walking up steep hills..

He's always been a bit of an *anti-climb Max*!

105

What did the secretive bricklayer who was in prison want?

To be a *free mason*!

106

Where did the computer go to dance?

The *disc-o!*

107

Why did the dad get the blame for stealing a painting, even though he didn't do it?

He was *framed!*

108

What did the dad vicar use to improve his vegetable garden?

Lettuce spray!

109

Why did the boa constrictors go on a date?

Because they had a *crush* on each other!

110

What does a subservient fish know?

His *plaice!*

111

What does Charles Dickens keep in his spice rack?

The best of thymes, the worst of thymes!

112

What did the man do when his girlfriend
criticized his apartment?

He *knocked her flat*!

113

Why was the dad arrested for hanging around
too long at the circus?

For loitering *within a tent!*

114

What dog can jump higher than a building?

All of them, buildings can't jump!

115

How does a dad use to fix a broken tomato?

Tomato paste!

116

Why did the dad insist on having candles on
his birthday cake?

He wanted to make *light* of his age!

117

What did the dad at the garden café do when
he found a lot of coffee residue at the bottom
of his mug?

He called the *groundskeeper!*

118

Where does Santa go swimming?

The North *Pool!*

119

What washes up on tiny beaches?

Microwaves!

120

Did you hear about the earthquake in Washington?

It was the government's *fault*!

121

Did you hear about the feline dad who entered the milk-drinking race?

He won by five *laps!*

122

Why did the dad butcher refuse to sell half a rabbit?

He didn't want to *split hares!*

123

How do fairy tail creatures keep their rhythm?

With a metro-*gnome!*

124

What do you call an angry dad who has gotten permanent green marker on his face?

The Indelible Hulk!

125

Why did the barman-dad invite a drunk baseball player to the bar?

Someone asked for a *pitcher full of beer!*

126

Why don't miner-dads wear helmets when they go underground?

They don't want to feel *lightheaded!*

127

What happened to the dentist-dad who joined the army?

He became a *drill instructor!*

128

Did you hear about the two monastery men who opened up a seafood takeout?

One was the *fish friar*, the other was the *chip monk!*

129

What is a burglar-dad's favorite way of breaking in?

Intruder window!

130

Why do artists constantly feel cold?

Because they're surrounded by *drafts!*

131

What do you call a group of angry drivers in an
Egyptian traffic jam?

Tootin-car-men!

132

What do you call a wolf that can catch a deer
with either paw?

Bambidextrous!

133

What did the clown-dad do when he was fired
from the circus without cause?

He sued for *funfair dismissal!*

134

Why did the lost dad lose his job at the massage parlor?

He *rubbed every body up the wrong way!*

135

What happened when the dad got stuck on his horse at the riding school?

His friends *derided* him!

136

What hairstyle do sea captains hate?

Crew cuts!

137

What do you get when you divide the circumference of a jack-o-lantern by its diameter?

Pumpkin Pi!

138

Why did the bankrupt dad move to France?

He had nothing *Toulouse!*

139

What is the shortest month?

May, *it only has three letters!*

140

What did the dad spider do when he was in the corn field?

He made *cob* webs!

141

What do you call a dad named Lee that no one talks to?

Lonely!

142

Why couldn't the pirate-dad play cards?

Because he was sitting on the *deck!*

143

Why do cows send so many text messages?

They like sending each other *e-moo-jis!*

144

Did you hear about the farmer dad who had 100 cows?

He thought he only had 97 but then he *rounded them up!*

145

How do mountains stay warm in winter?

Snowcaps!

146

How do you know when the moon is going broke?

When it's down to a *quarter*!

147

What do you call two people who've lost their psychic abilities?

Pair-a-normals!

148

What did the dad shop assistant do when a customer said he needed something for breaking up rocks?

He pointed to the tool isle and said "Take your *pick!*"

149

Why was the ghost-dad surprised when his reanimated wife got home at 11pm?

He didn't *ex-specter* until midnight!

150

Why wouldn't the dad close down his hay selling business?

He was clutching at *straws!*

151

What did the dad say when a customer asked "Waiter, will my pizza be long?"

"No sir, it will be round!"

152

Why were the dad's letters damp when they were delivered?

They had postage *dew!*

153

Why did the dad cross a dog with a hen?

He wanted *pooched eggs!*

154

Why do dragons sleep during the day?

So they can fight *knights!*

155

Where does a sick cow go if he needs some medicine?

To the *farm-acy!*

156

Why did the Buddhist refuse pain killers when he had his tooth pulled?

He wanted to transcend *dental medication*!

157

Why did the dad refuse to let his cat out of the house?

He heard there was a *purr snatcher* on the lose!

158

Why do old people tell the worst jokes?

Because they're *groan-ups!*

159

Why did the dad have his potato gun taken away by the army?

It was a weapon of *mash* destruction!

160

What do you call a mosquito that backpacks around Europe?

An *itch-hiker!*

161

What happened when the astronaut broke the law of gravity?

He got a *suspended* sentence!

162

Why did the orange lose the race?

He ran out of *juice!*

163

Why did the dad who was studying to be a surgeon rip the last page out of his textbook?

He wanted to practice removing an *appendix!*

164

Who did the dad call when he found a ghost in his hotel?

An *inn specter!*

165

How do trains hear?

With *engine-ears*!

166

Why did the first attempt at building the
Channel Tunnel rail line fail?

**The builders realized they had *Britain* off
more than they could *choo!***

167

What do you call an overweight alien?

An extra *cholesterol!*

168

Why don't dads enjoy television shows about origami?

Because they're *pa-per view!*

169

Why did the dad wear a cap with a large peak to work when he'd be using dangerous machinery?

He was told he would need a *supervisor!*

170

Why did the army-dad flush the toilet?

It was his *doody!*

171

What does a dad eat when he's cold and angry?

A *brrrgrrr!*

172

Why should you never go to a cheap dad eye surgeon?

They cut *corneas!*

173

Why should you never buy a cardboard belt?

It's just a *waist of paper!*

174

Why was the dad scared when he heard of a disease that was found in soft butter?

He heard it *spread easily!*

175

What do you call a funny mountain?

Hill-arious!

176

What's the difference between an angry magician and an Italian barber?

One is a *raving showman*, and the other is a *shaving Roman!*

177

Why do fairy tale creatures often get indigestion?

They're always *goblin* their food!

178

Why do dad hairdressers offend a lot of people?

Because they make a lot of *cutting remarks!*

179

What do you call two guys hanging on a window?

Kurt and Rod!

180

What did the dad say when the car park attendant told him he had to move his car because it was badge holders only?

"But I have got a bad shoulder!"

181

I once met a sunbathing mathematician who often strayed from the topic of conversation..

He was a real *tan gent!*

182

Why did the tall baseball player hate talking?

He was worried he had a *high-pitched* voice!

183

Why did the chewing gum cross the road?

It was stuck on the chicken's foot!

184

Why did the dad turn down the job at the
window blinds factory?

He thought the business sounded *shady!*

185

What did the bartender say when a group of
rowdy fonts walked into the bar?

We don't want your *type* in here*!*

186

How do you know when a dad chemist has fallen asleep?

He stops *reacting!*

187

Why did the overweight dad go to the local paint store?

He heard it was the best place to get *thinner!*

188

What time is it when an elephant sits on your fence?

Time to get a new one!

189

What happened when the dad-racing-driver had a wheel failure?

He had to *retire*!

190

Why do hippies like camping so much?

Cause it's in tents, man!

191

What is the biggest kind of ant?

An *elephant!*

192

What is a dad-frog's favorite motto?

Time's fun when you're having flies!

193

Why didn't the dad get charged when he was
accused of stealing a badge?

They couldn't *pin* it on him!

194

What's the difference between a TV and a newspaper?

Ever tried swatting a fly with a TV?

195

Why did the cookie go to the doctor?

He was feeling *crumby!*

196

Why did the dad chop off the bottom of his trouser leg and send it to the library?

He thought it would be a *turn-up for the books!*

197

Where do sheep go to get their hair cut?

The *baa-baa!*

198

Why is Peter Pan always flying?

Because he *Neverlands!*

199

What do you call a parade of rabbits hopping backwards?

A *receding hare-line!*

200

Why did the dad buy a book full of puns?

He wanted to be well e-*quipped!*

THANK YOU!

I really hope you've had a great time
tormenting your friends and family
with these jokes!

If you've enjoyed this book, please tell the
world by leaving a review on **Amazon.com**!

Also please take a look at my other books,
designed to provide you with more good times
with your friends and loved ones:

Conversation Starters

Conversation Starters for Teens

Conversation Starters for Couples

What Would You Do?

Thanks again!

Made in the USA
Middletown, DE
17 December 2017